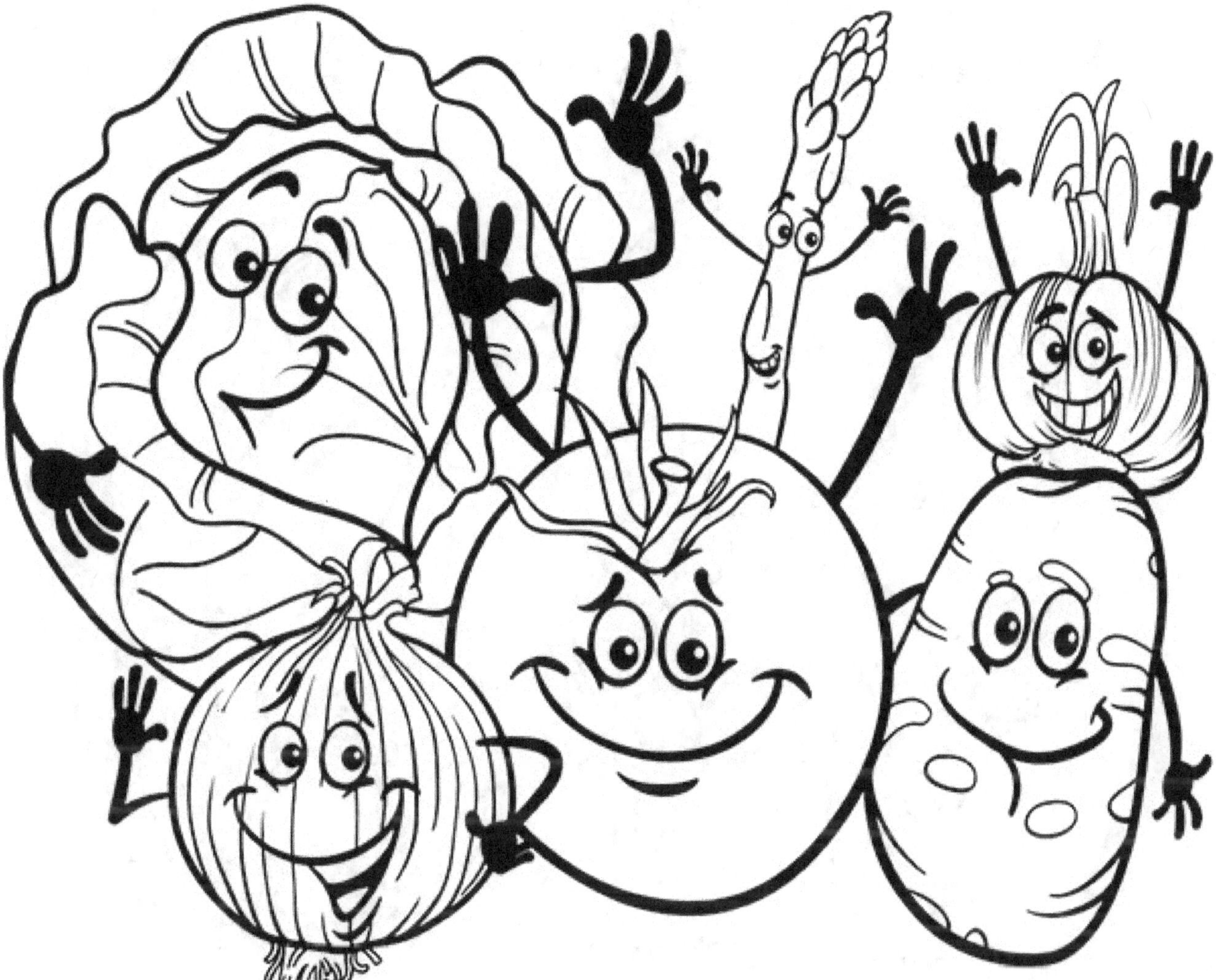

VEGETABLES

WE KEEP YOU

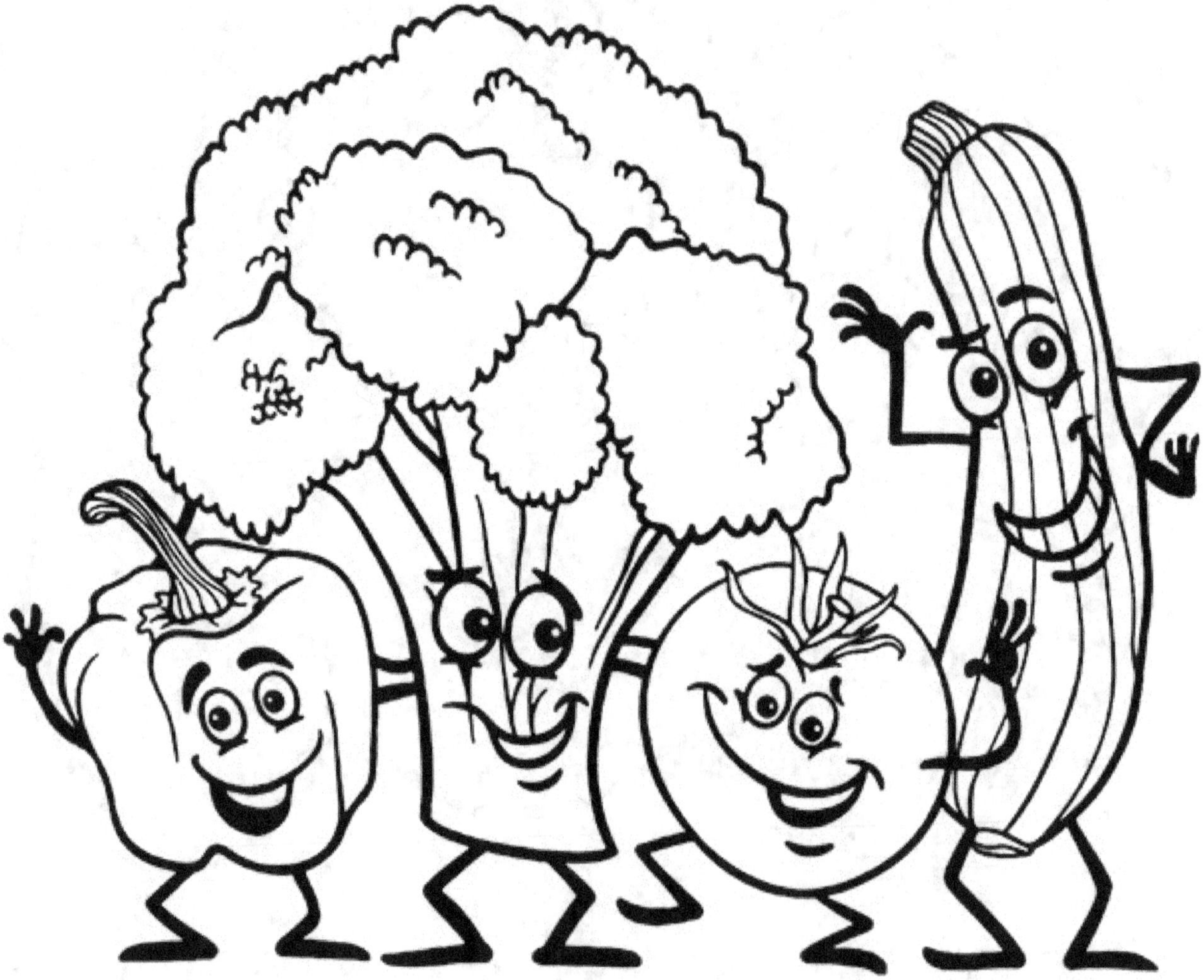

HEALTHY!

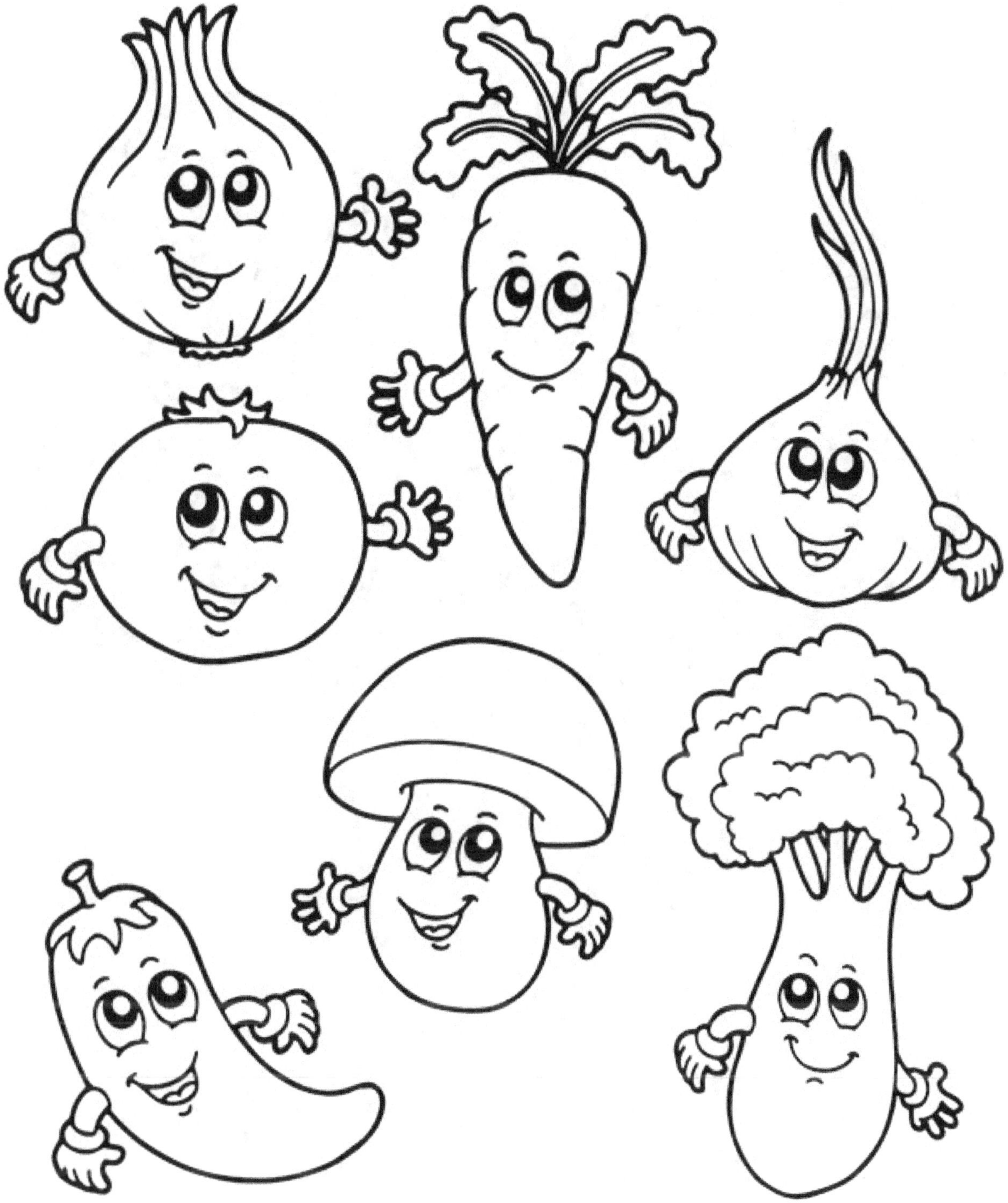

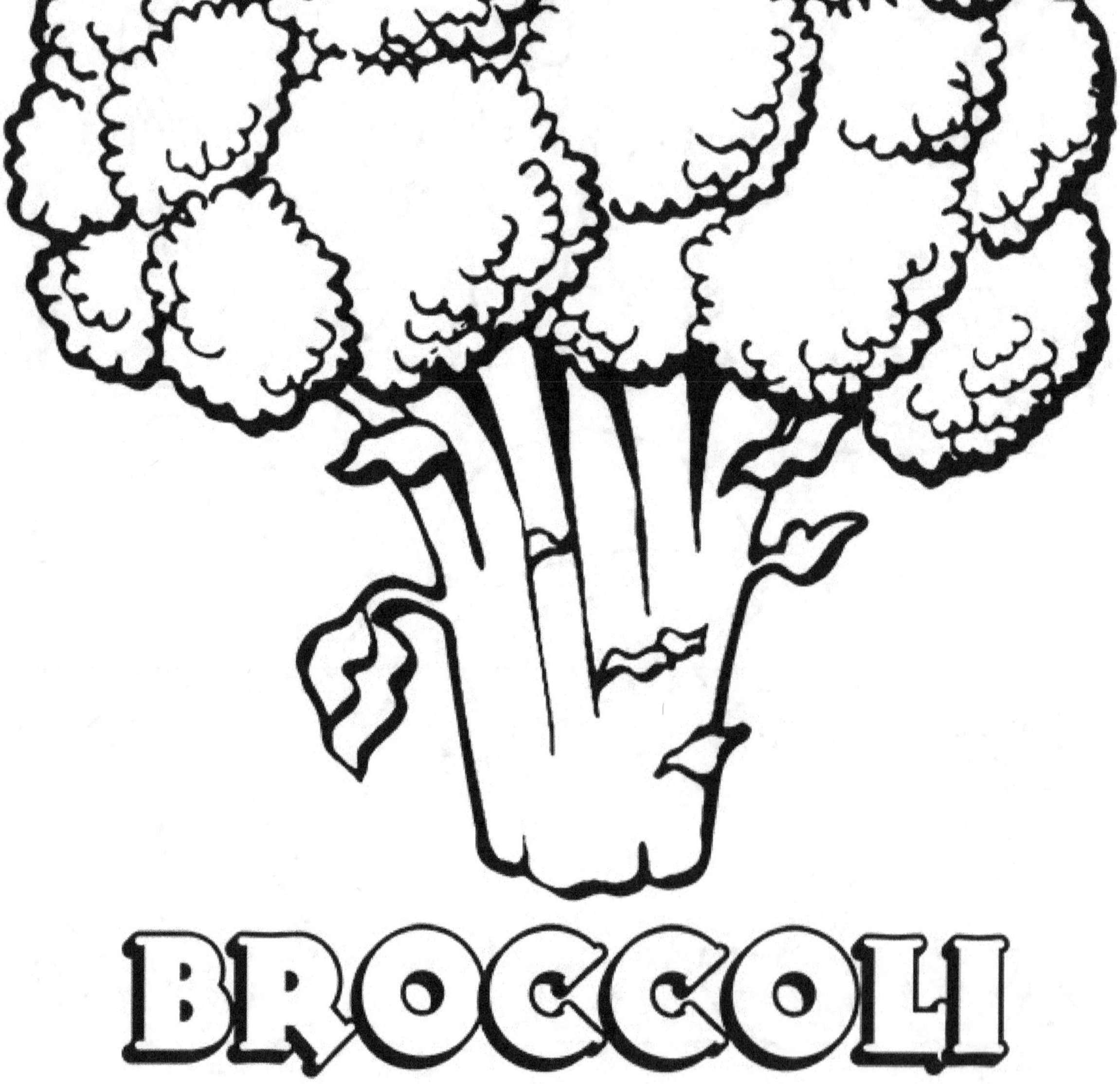

BROCCOLI

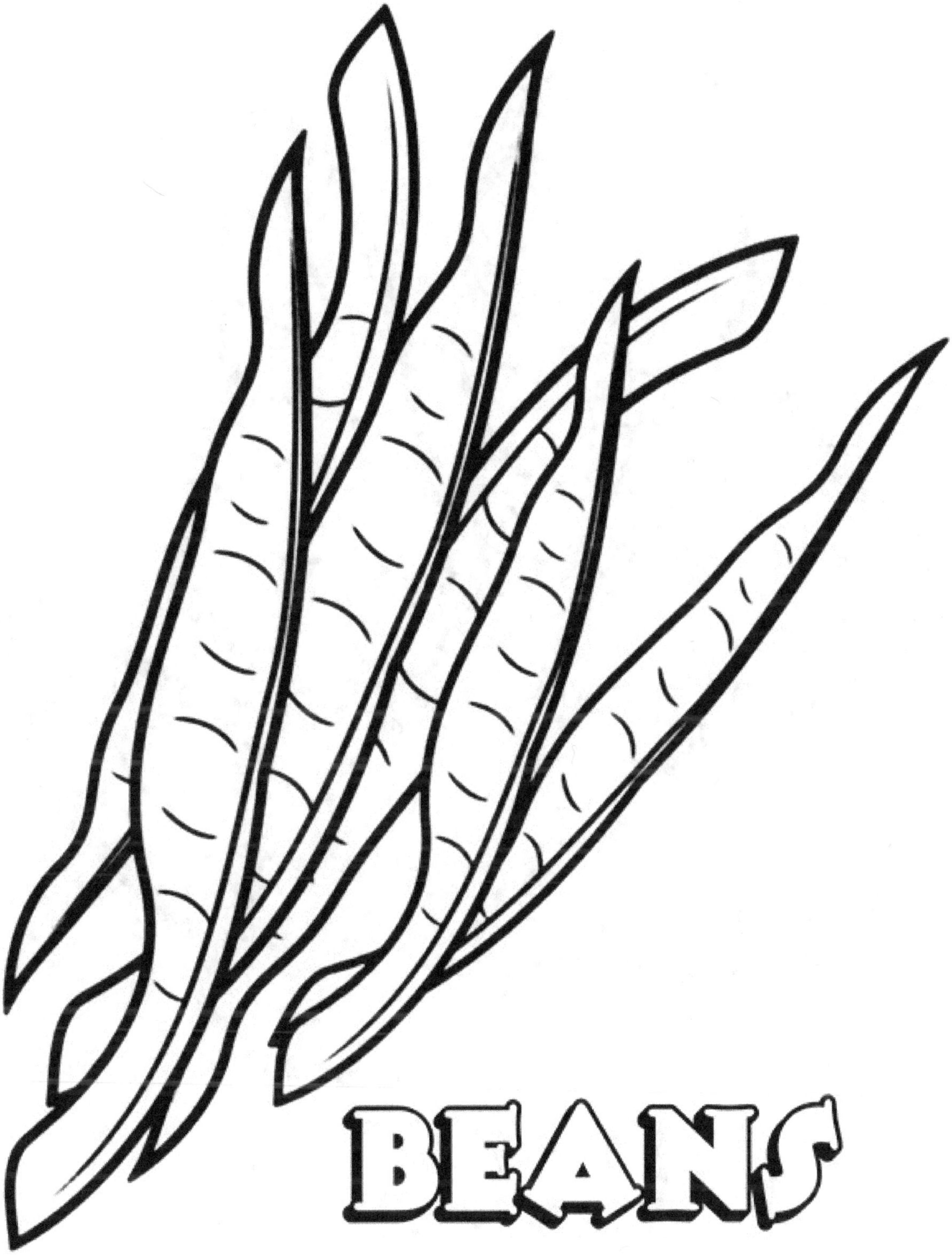
BEANS

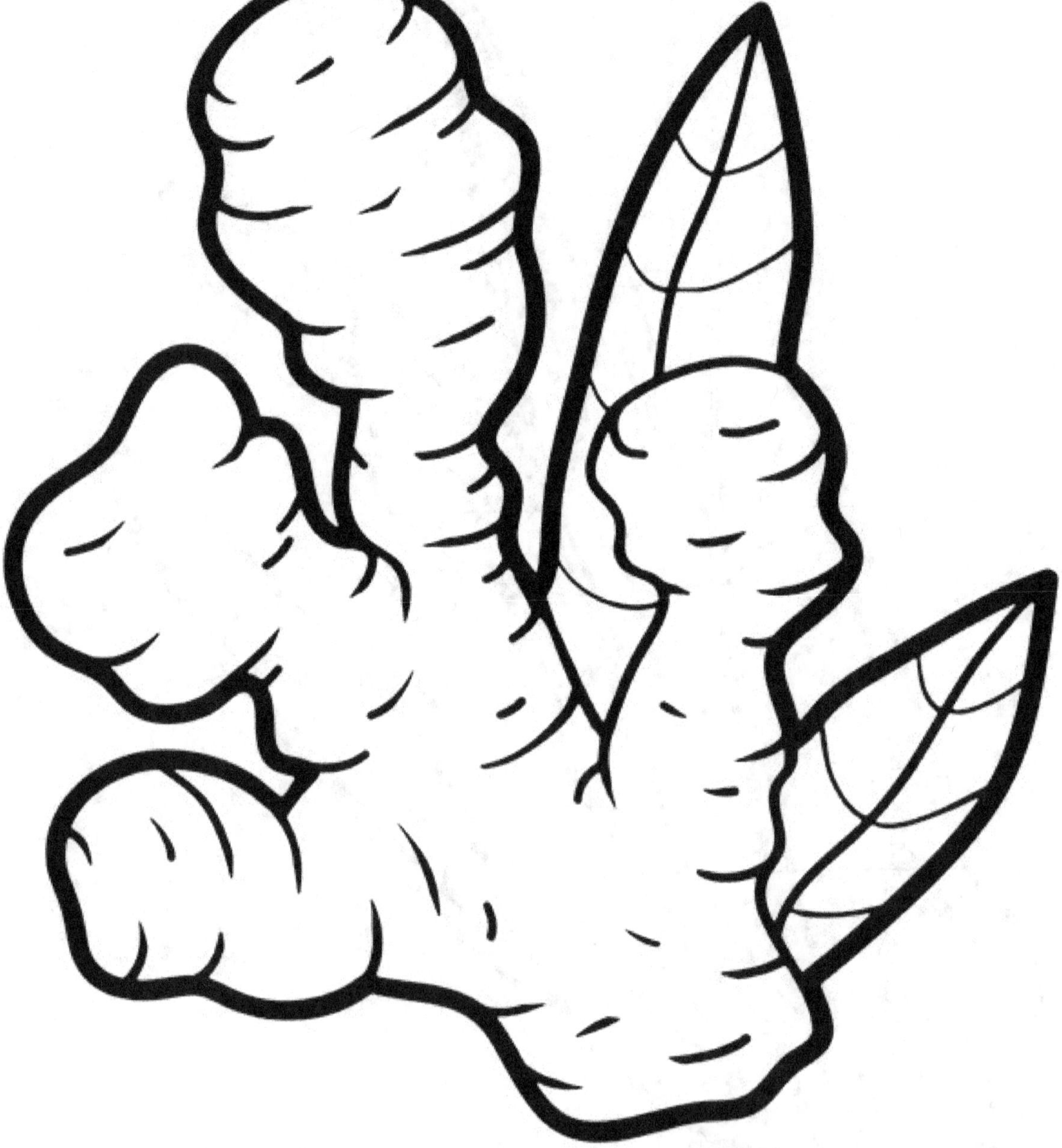

GINGER

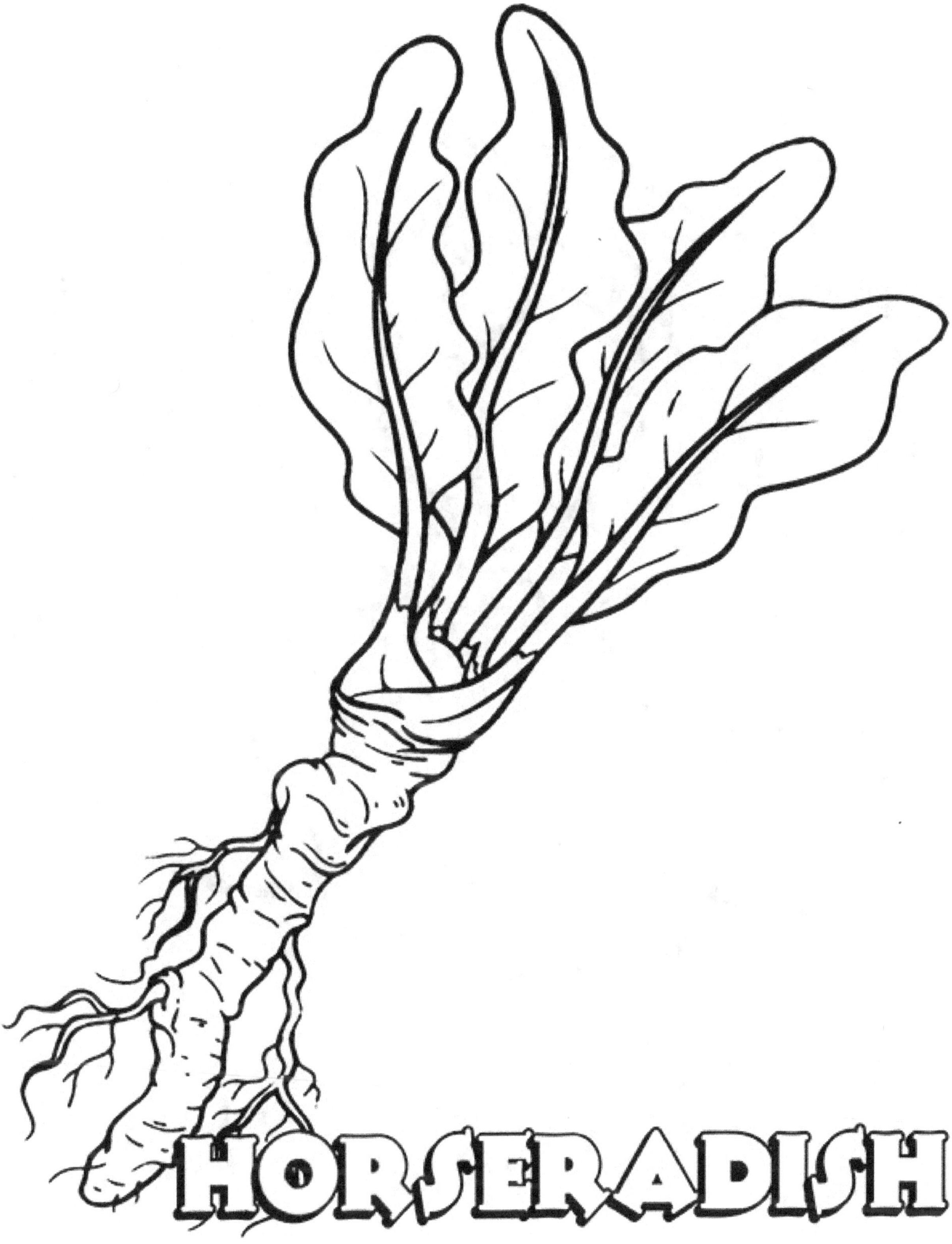

HORSERADISH

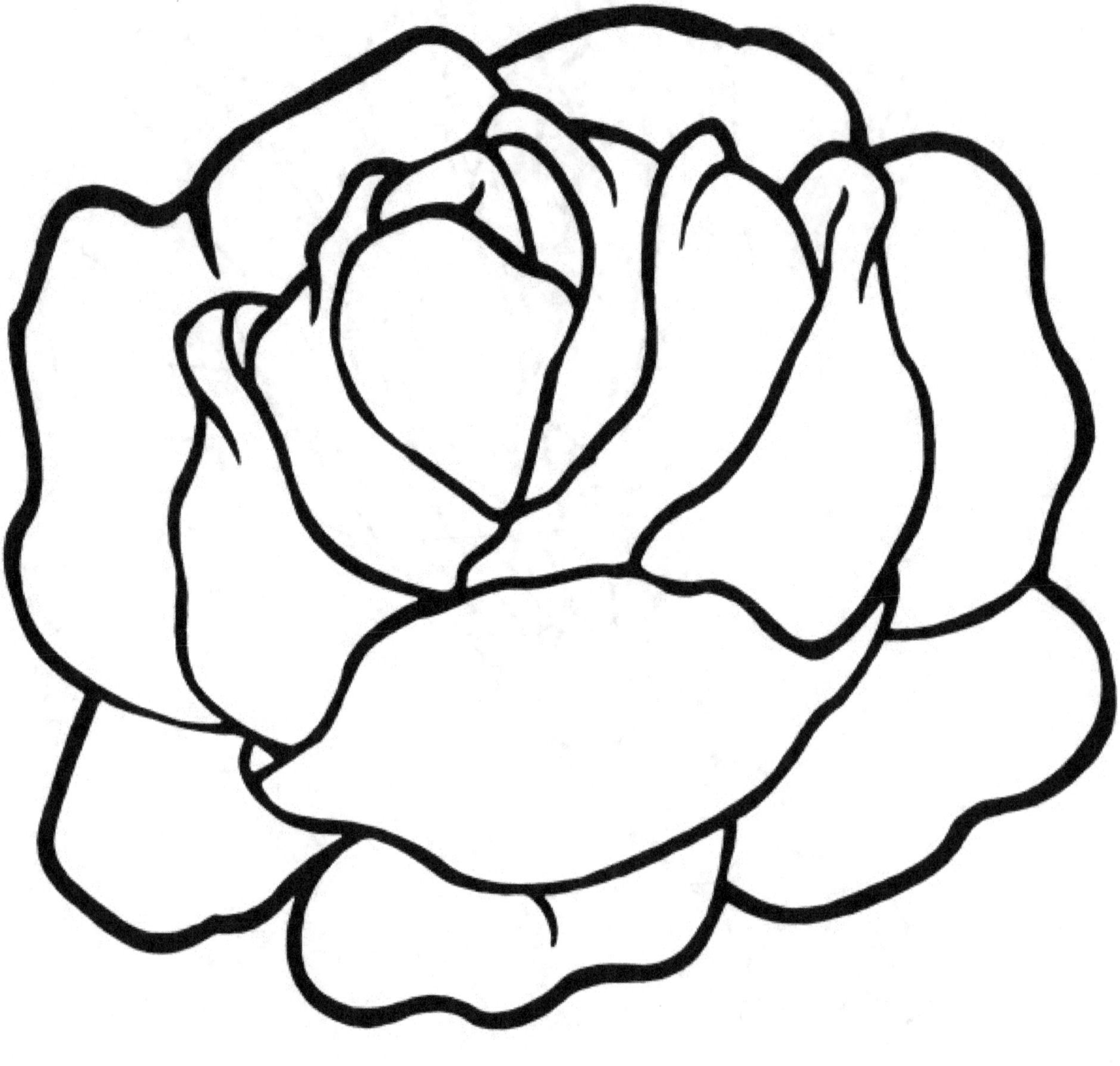

LETTUCE

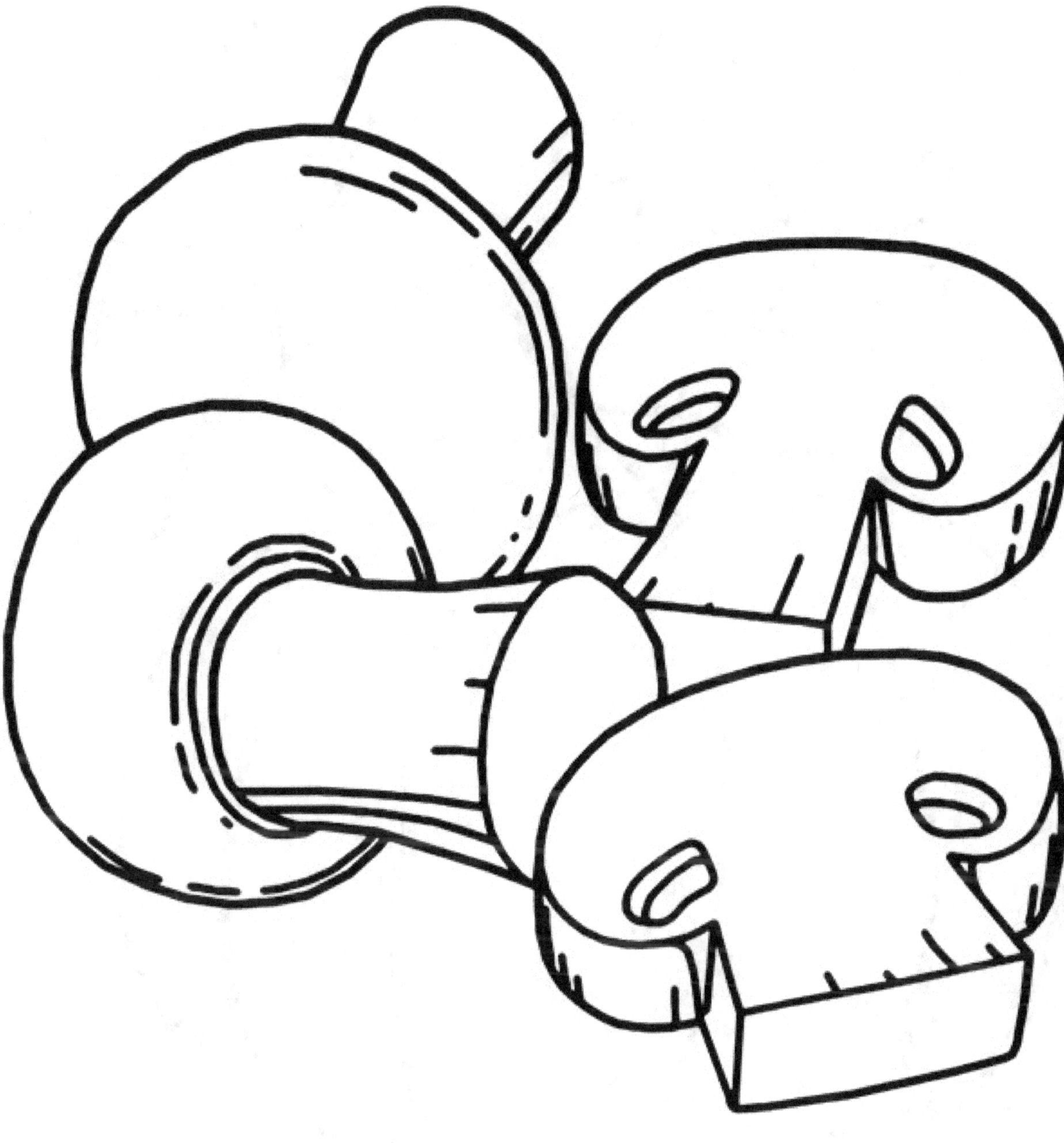

MUSHROOM

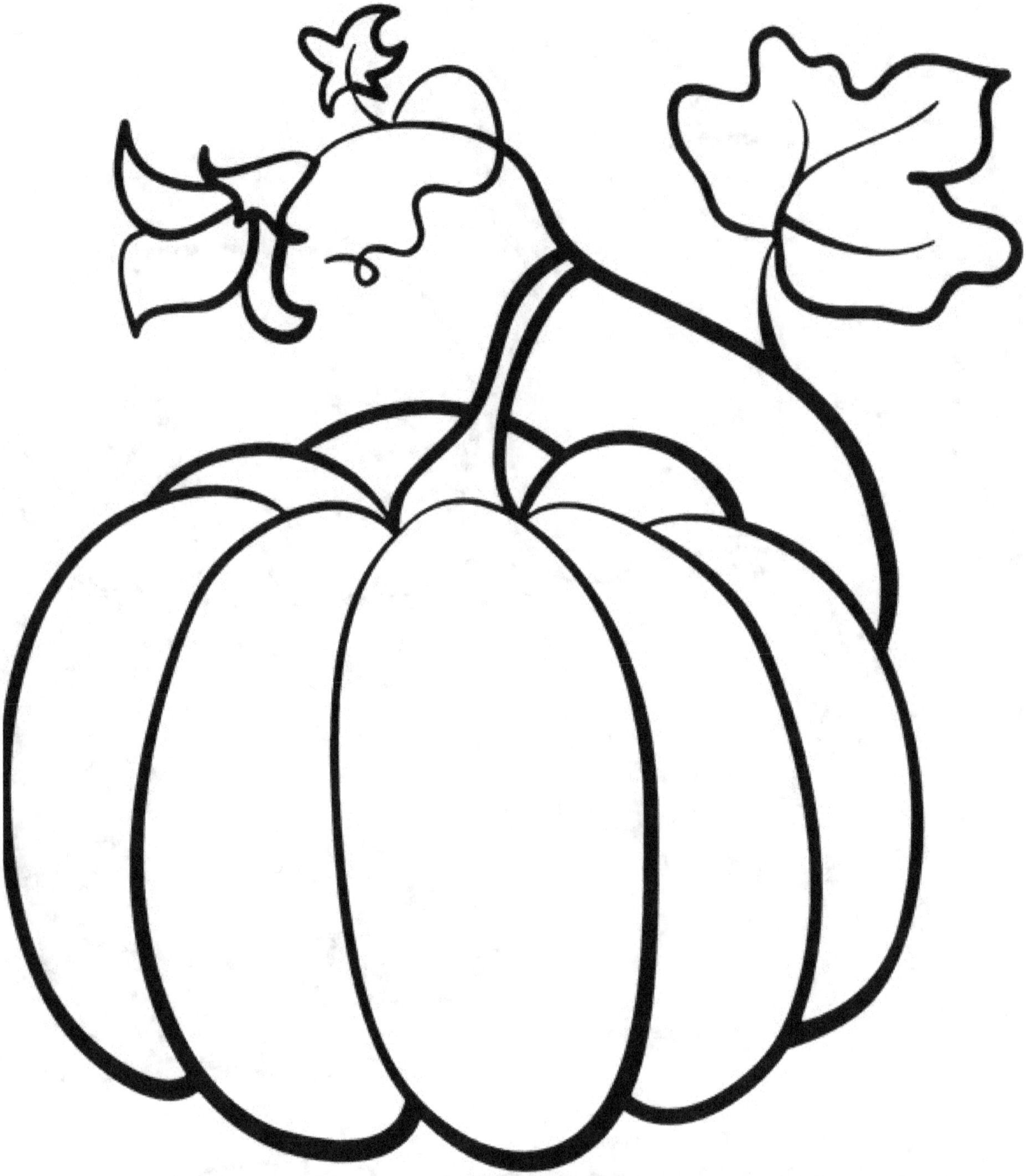

PUMPKIN

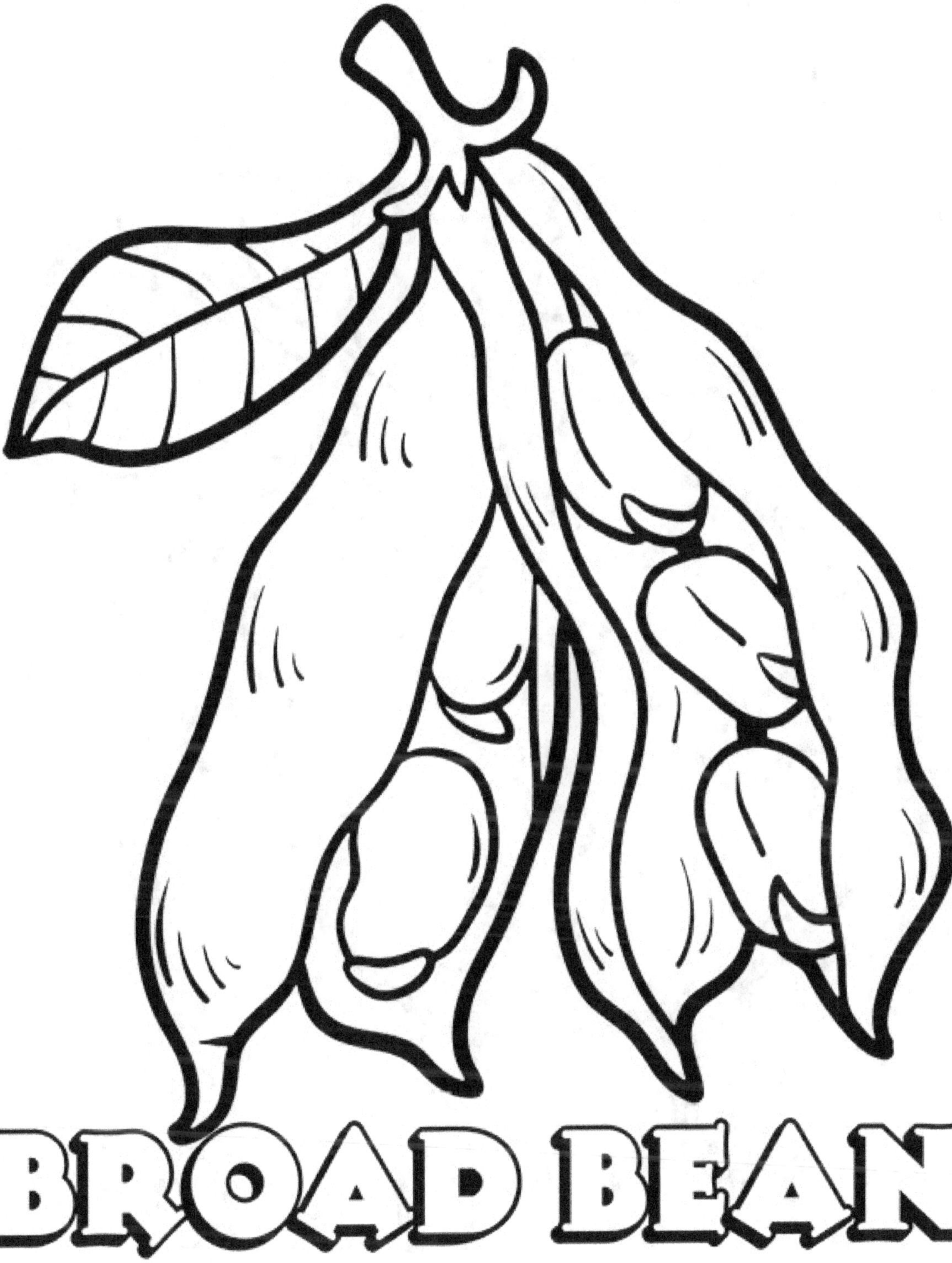

BROAD BEAN

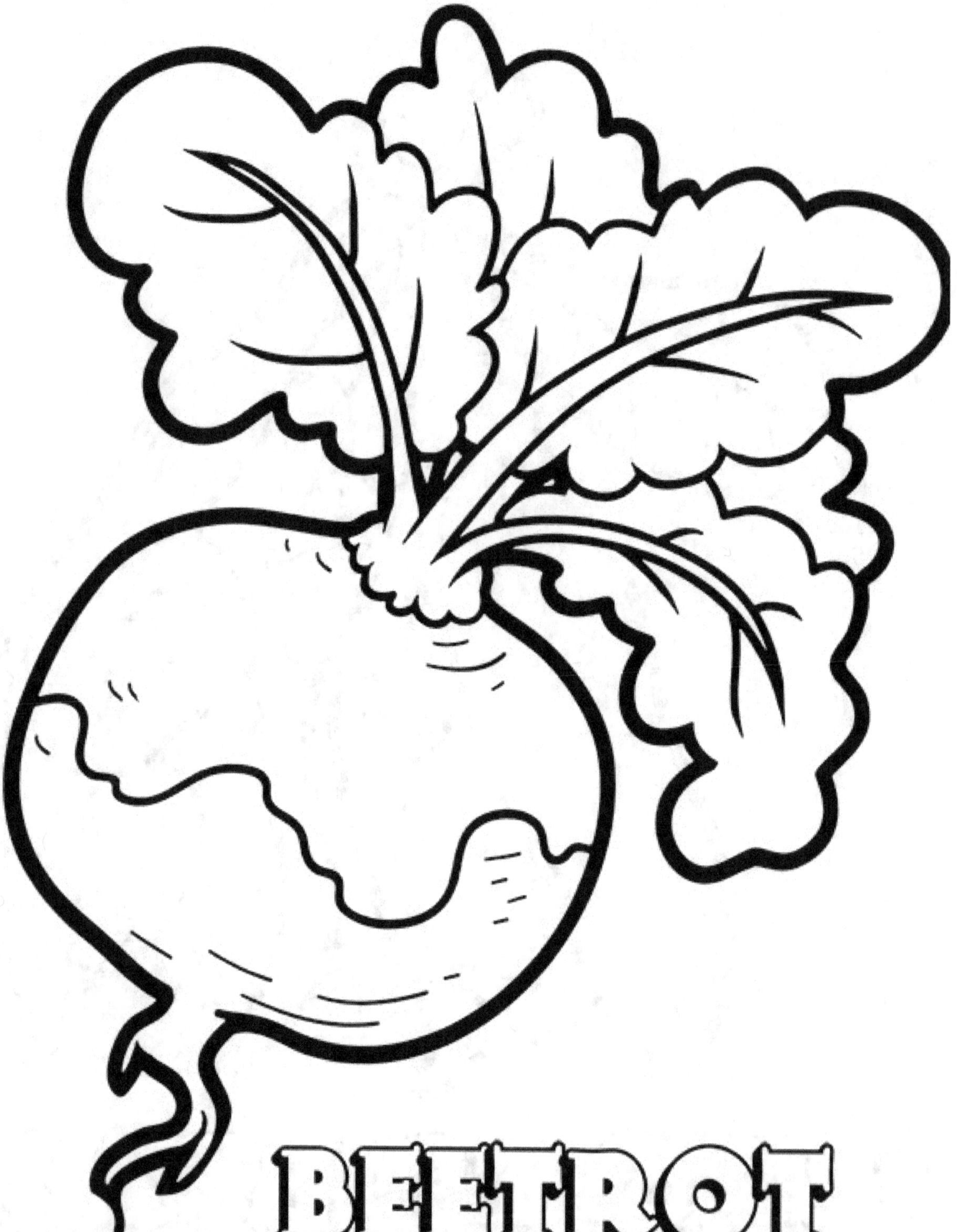

BEETROT

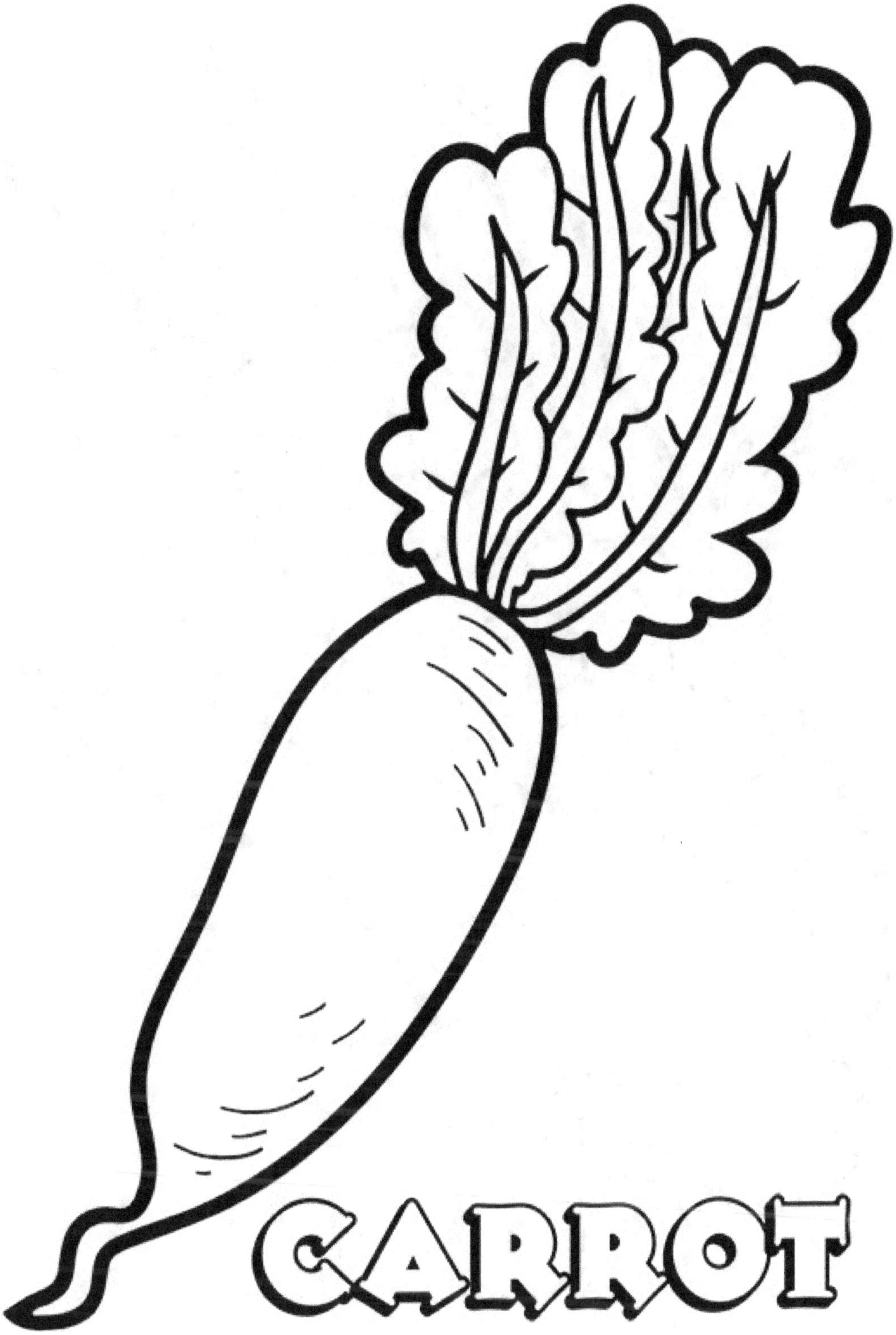

CARROT

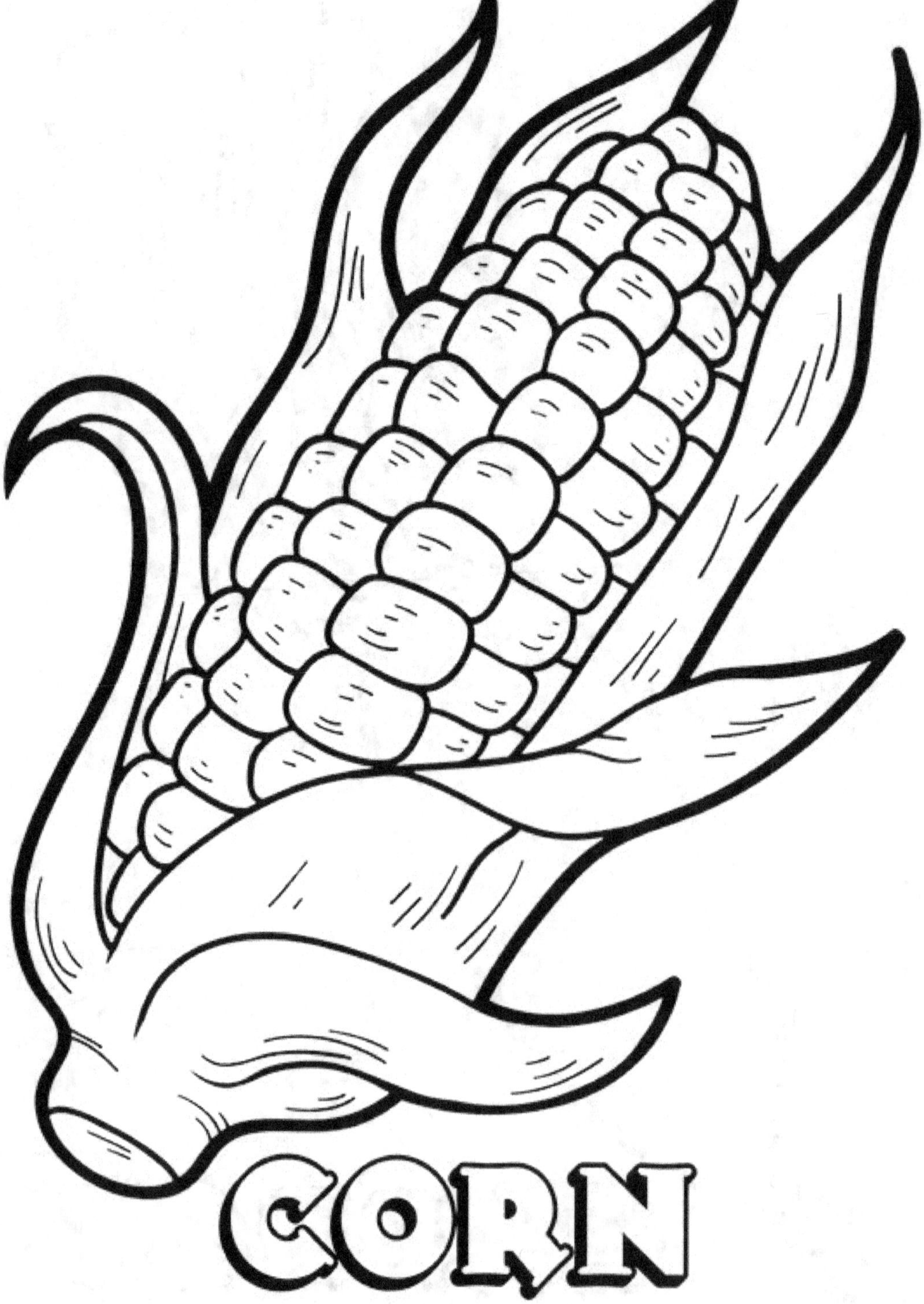

CORN

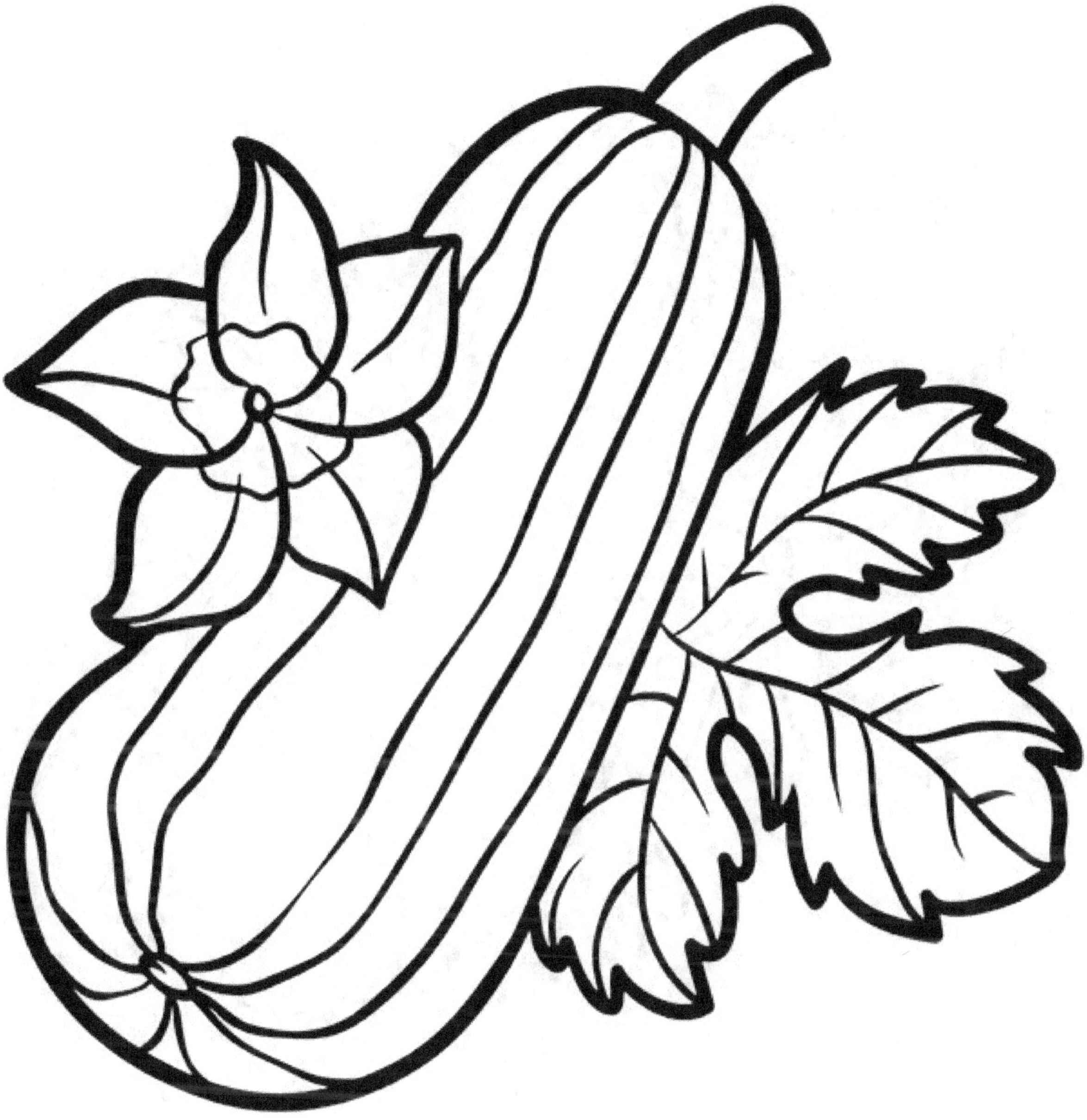

COURGETTE

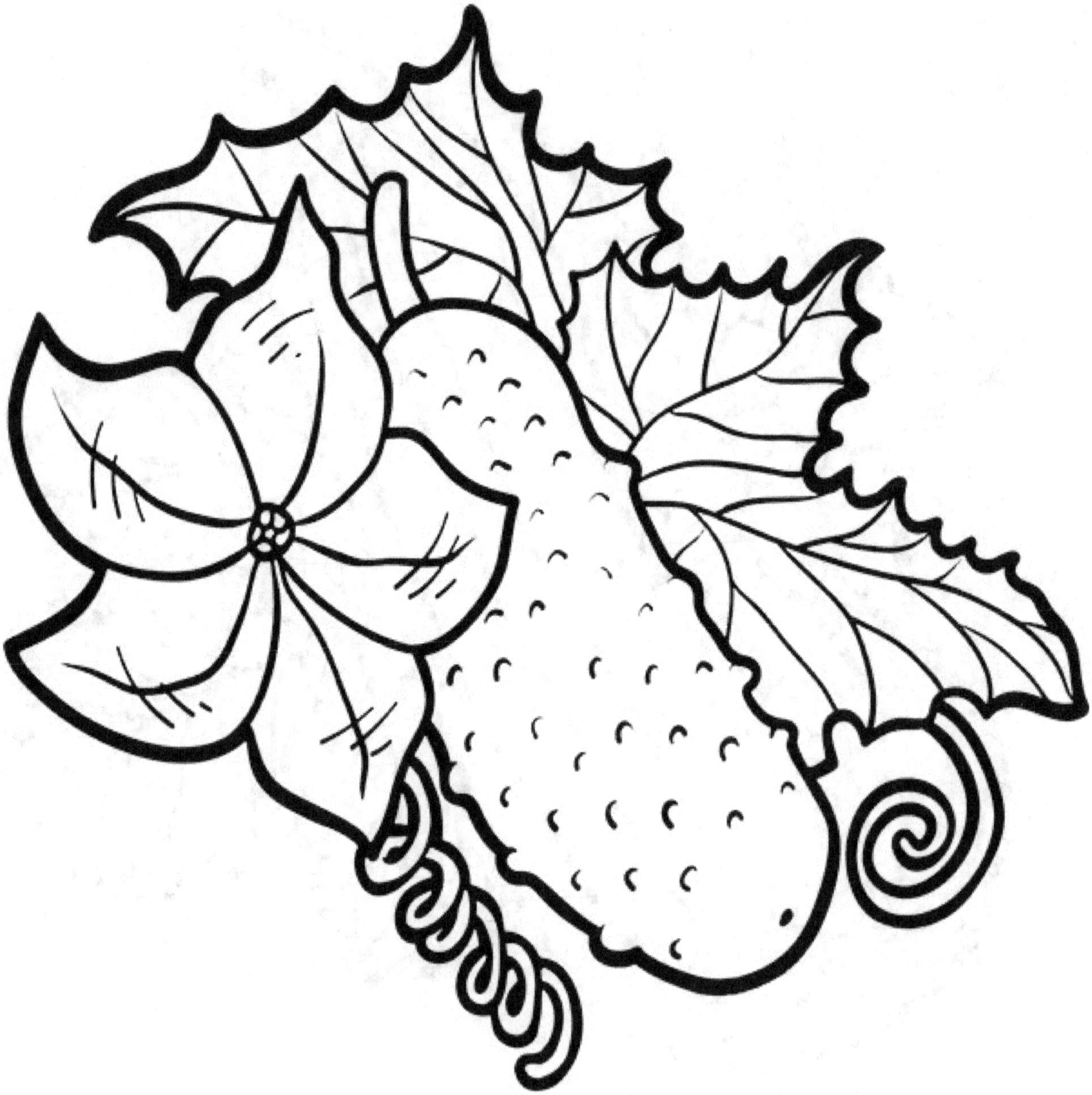

CUCUMBER

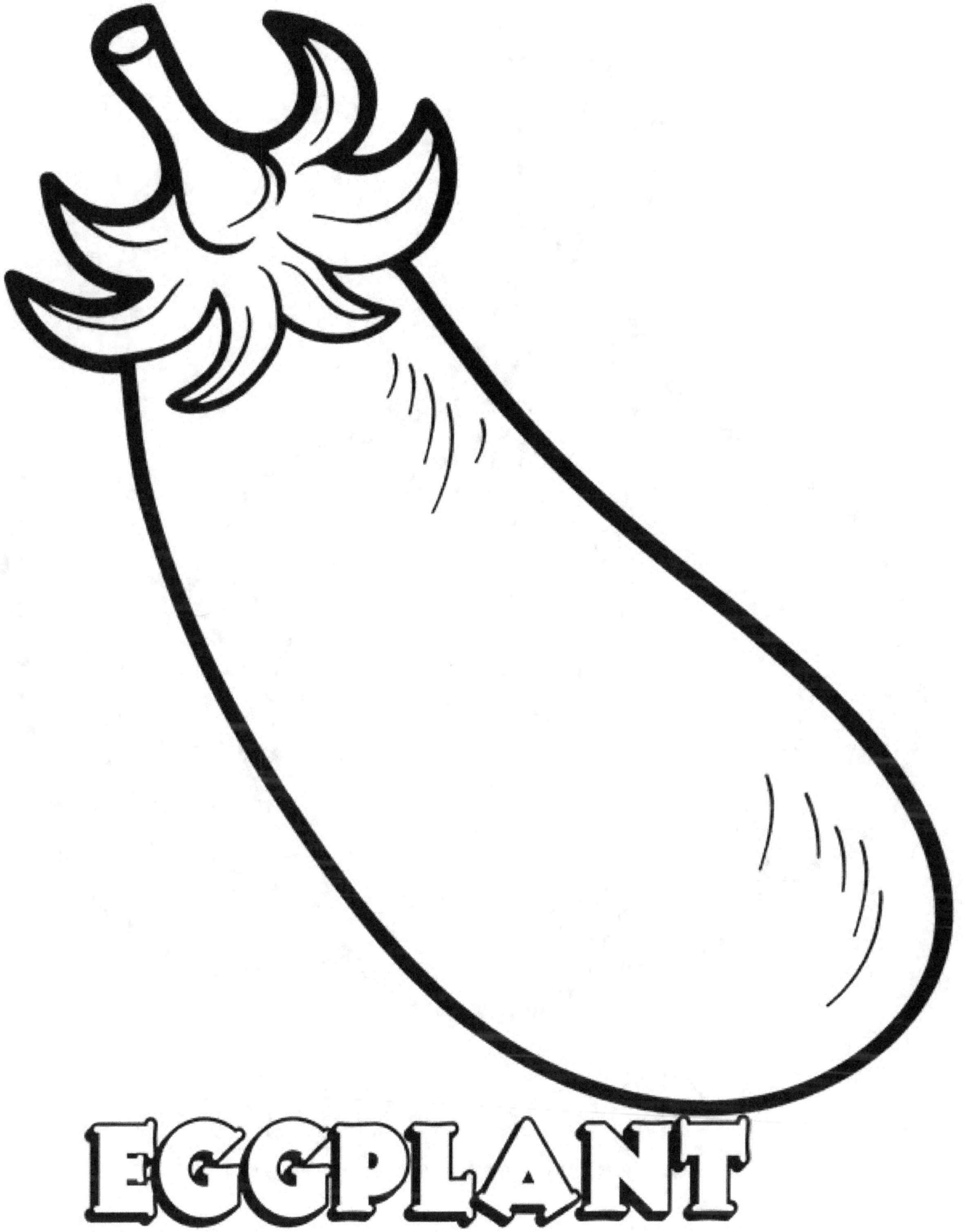

EGGPLANT

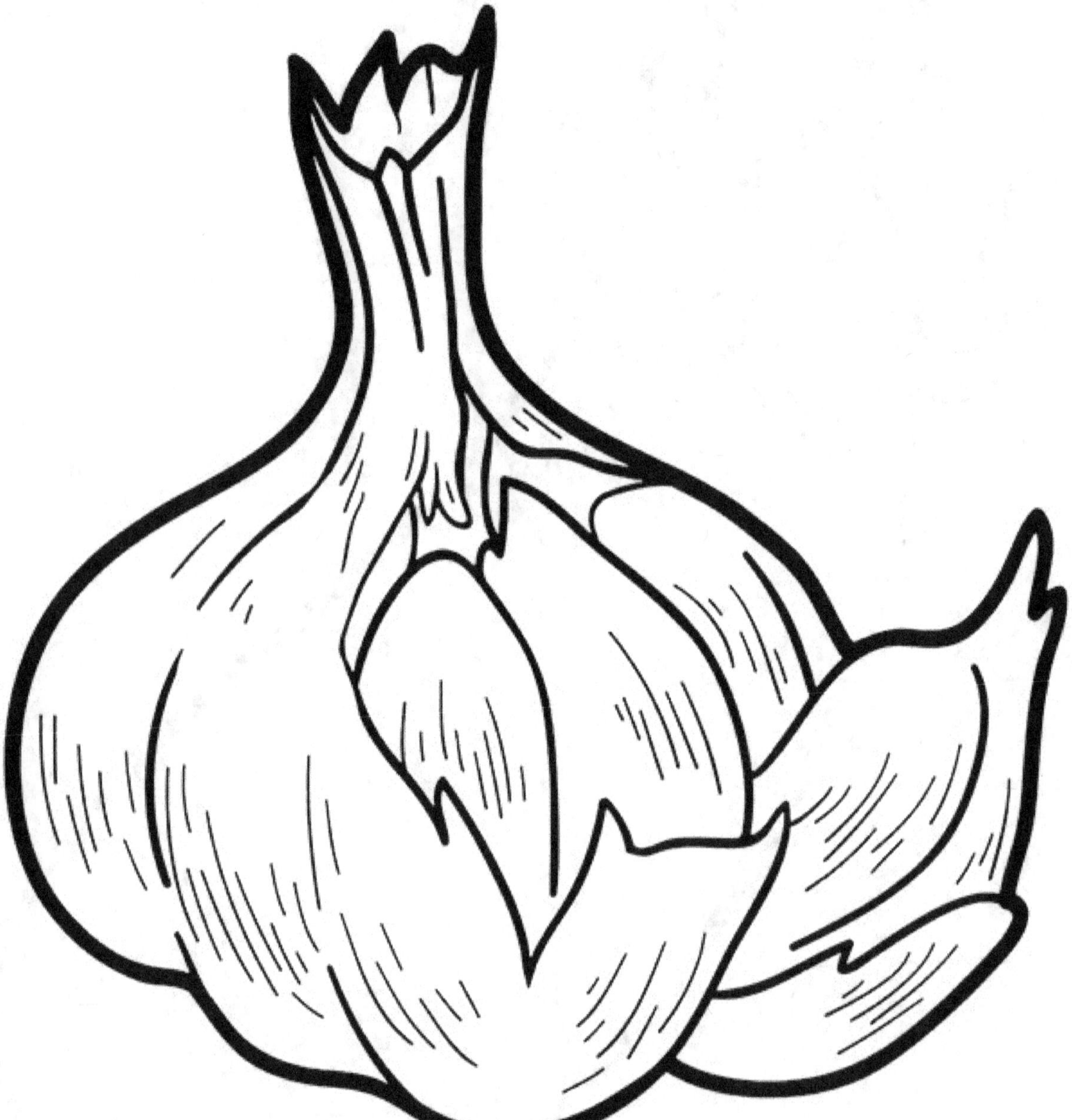

GARLIC

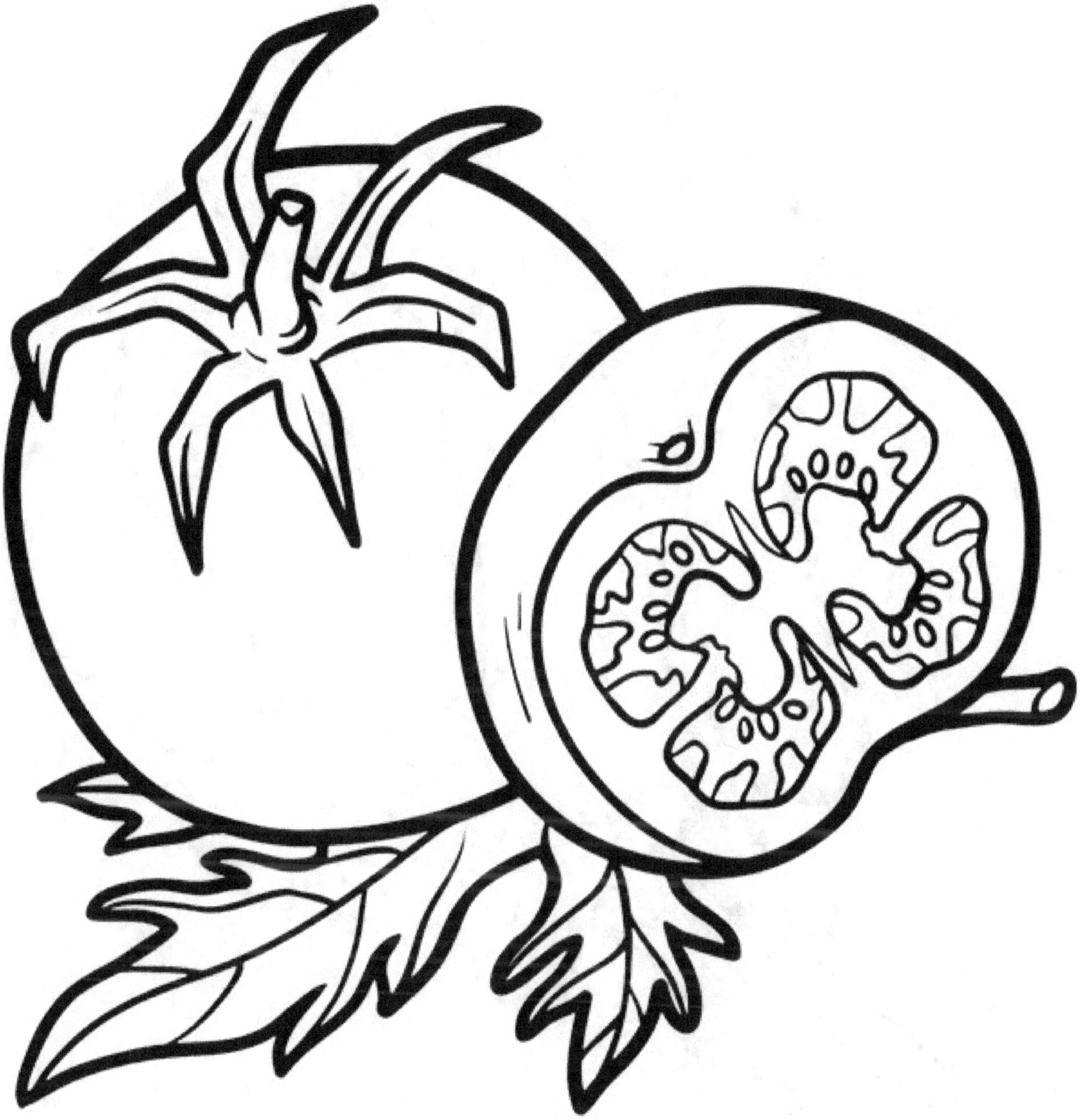

TOMATO

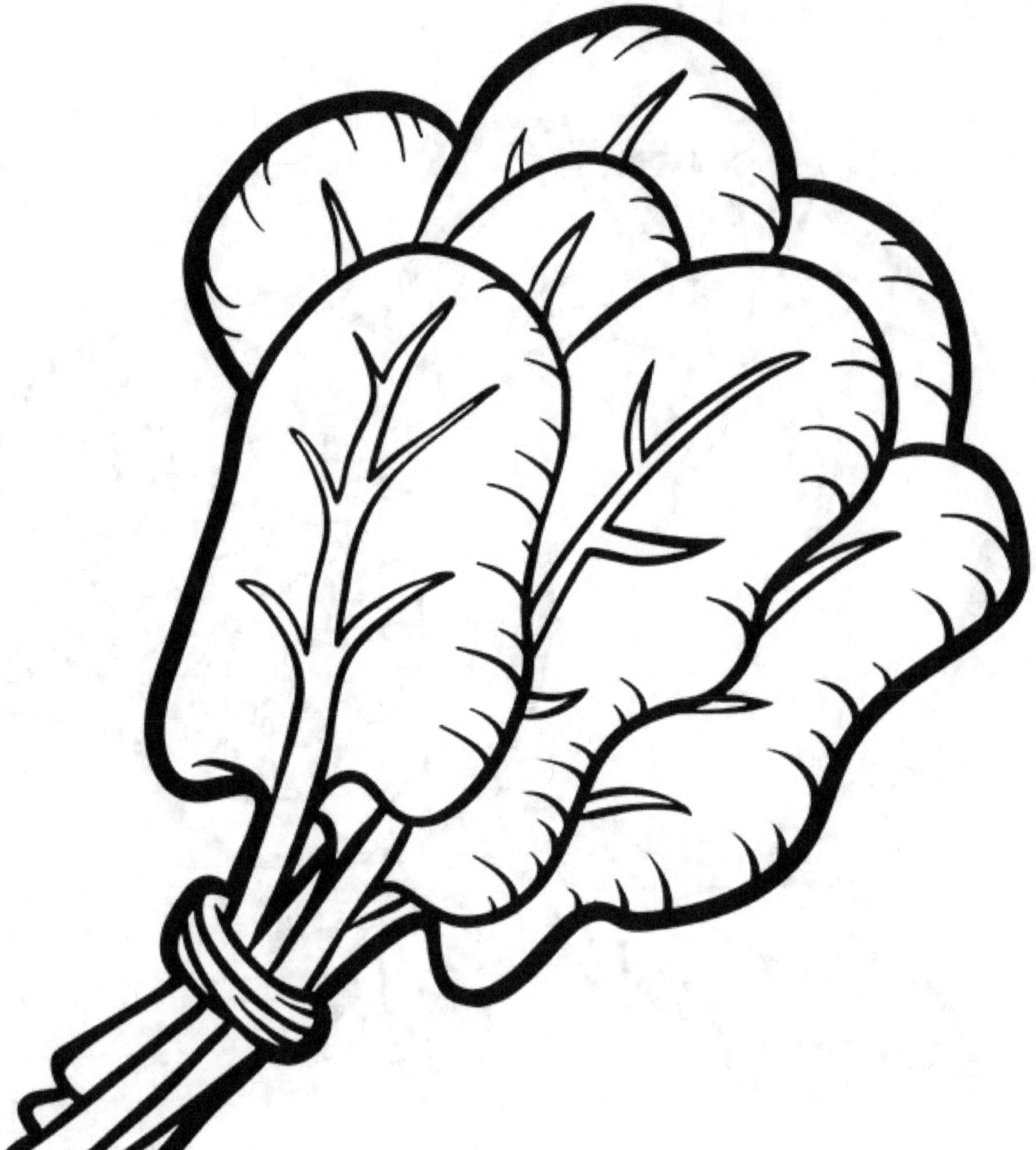

SPINACH

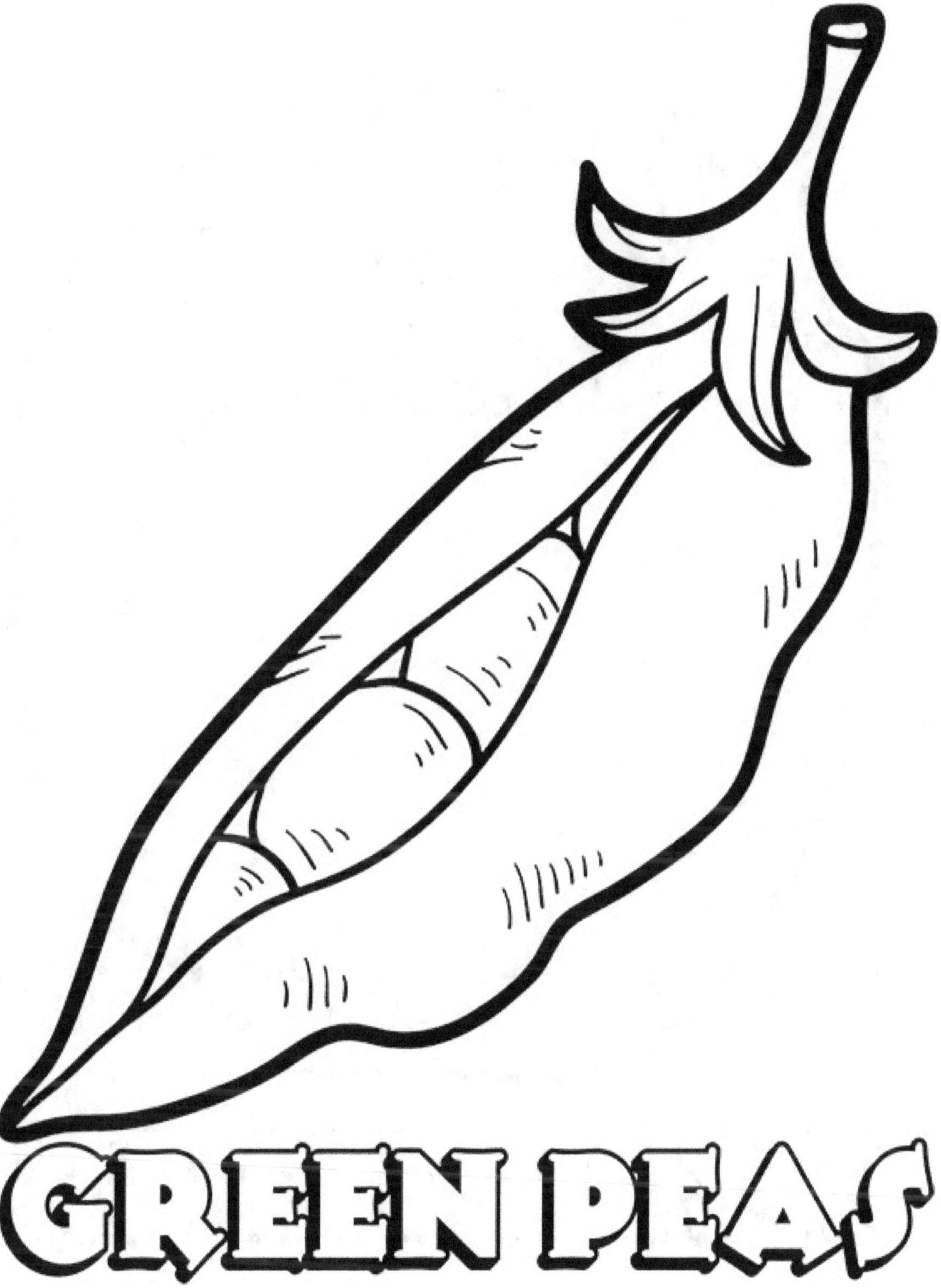

GREEN PEAS

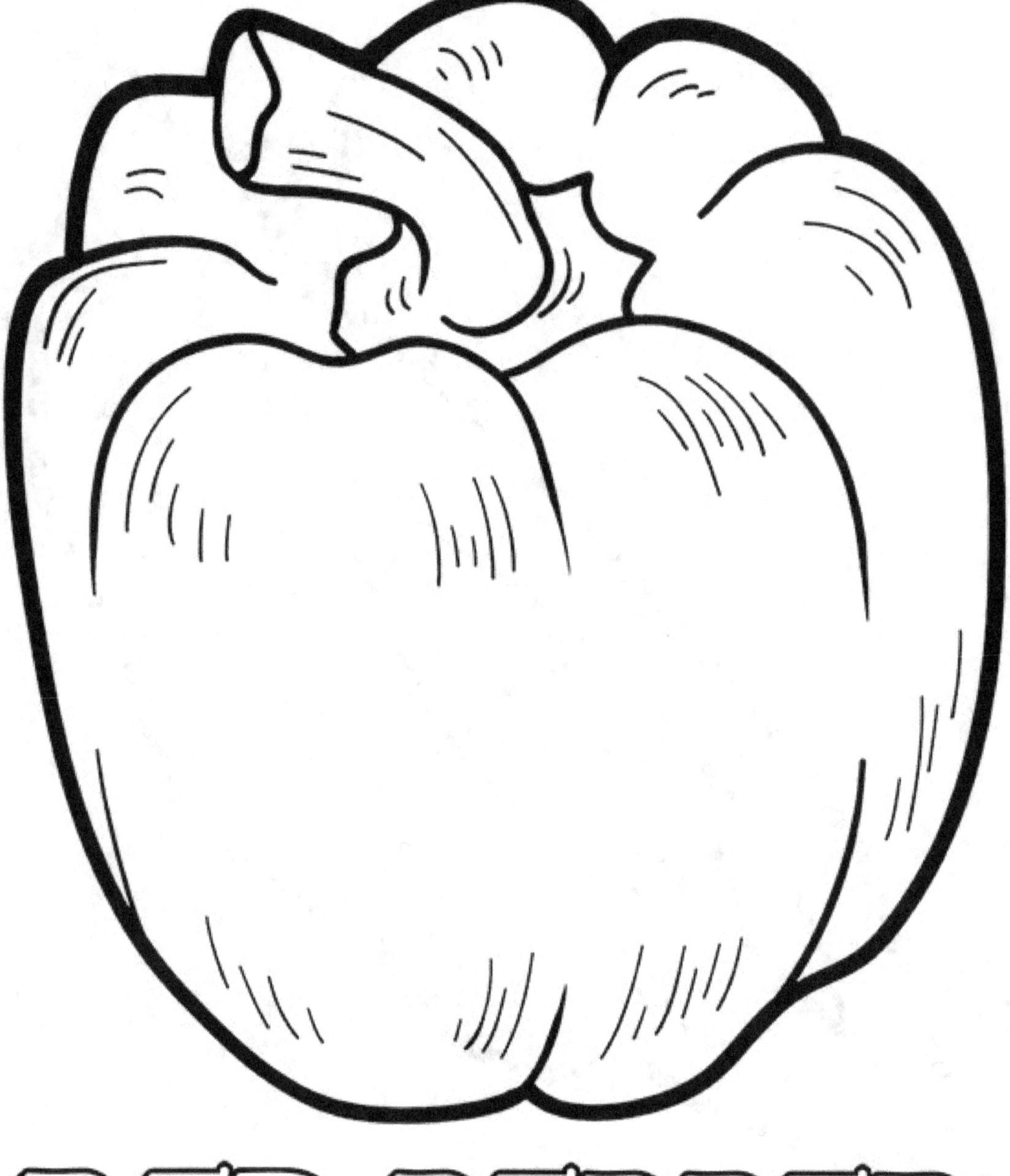

RED PEPPER

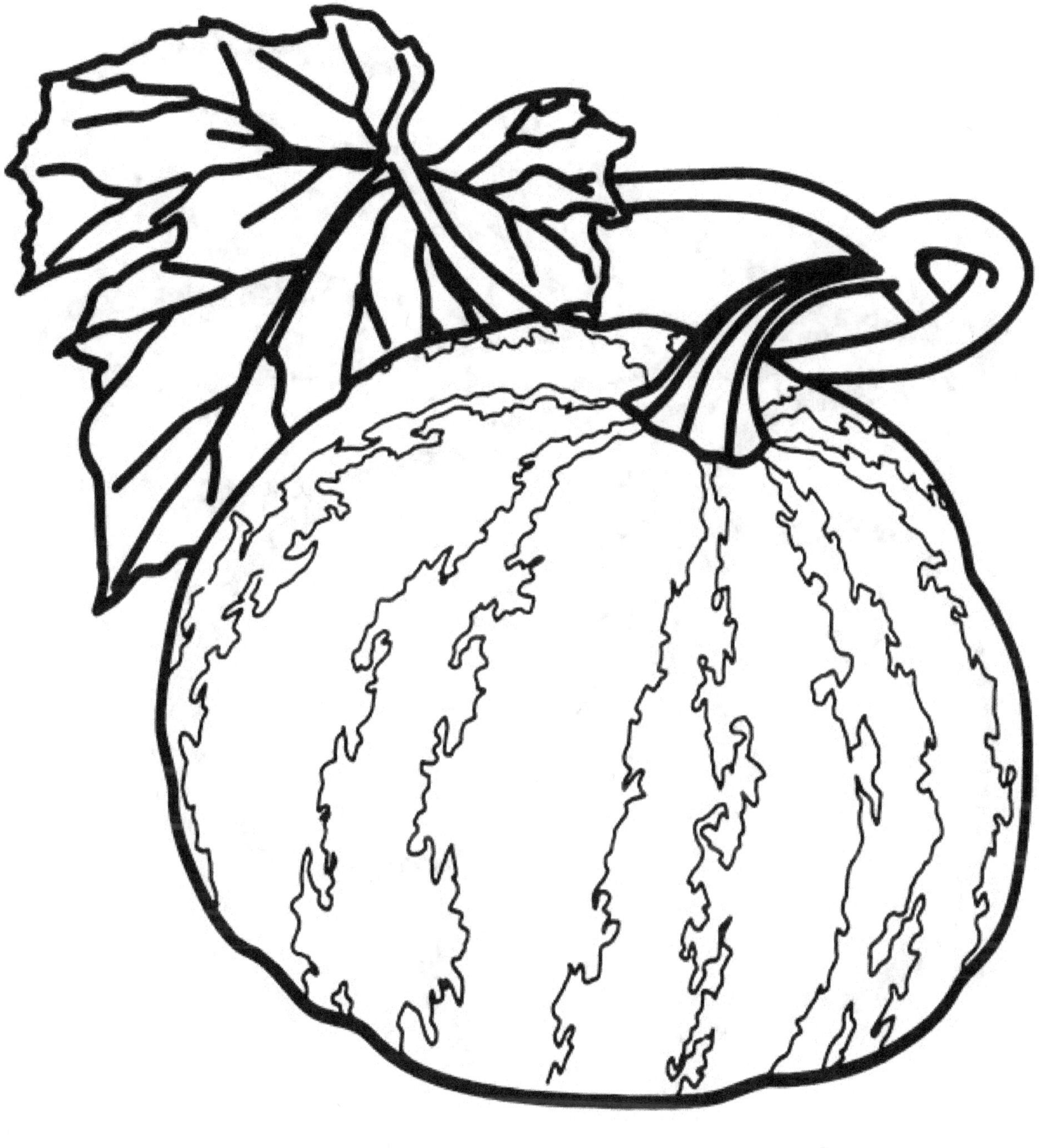

ROUND ZUCCHINI

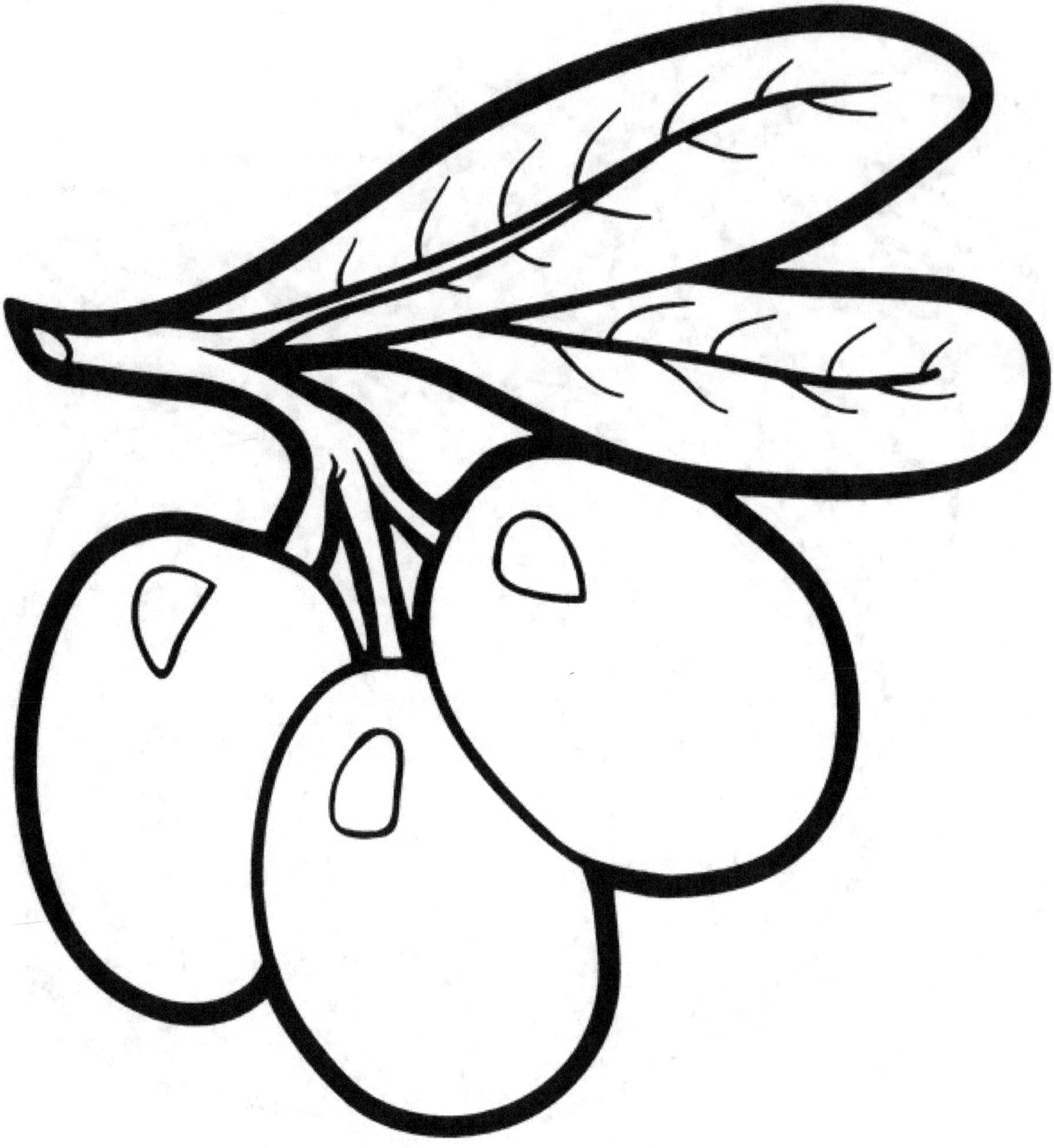

OLIVES

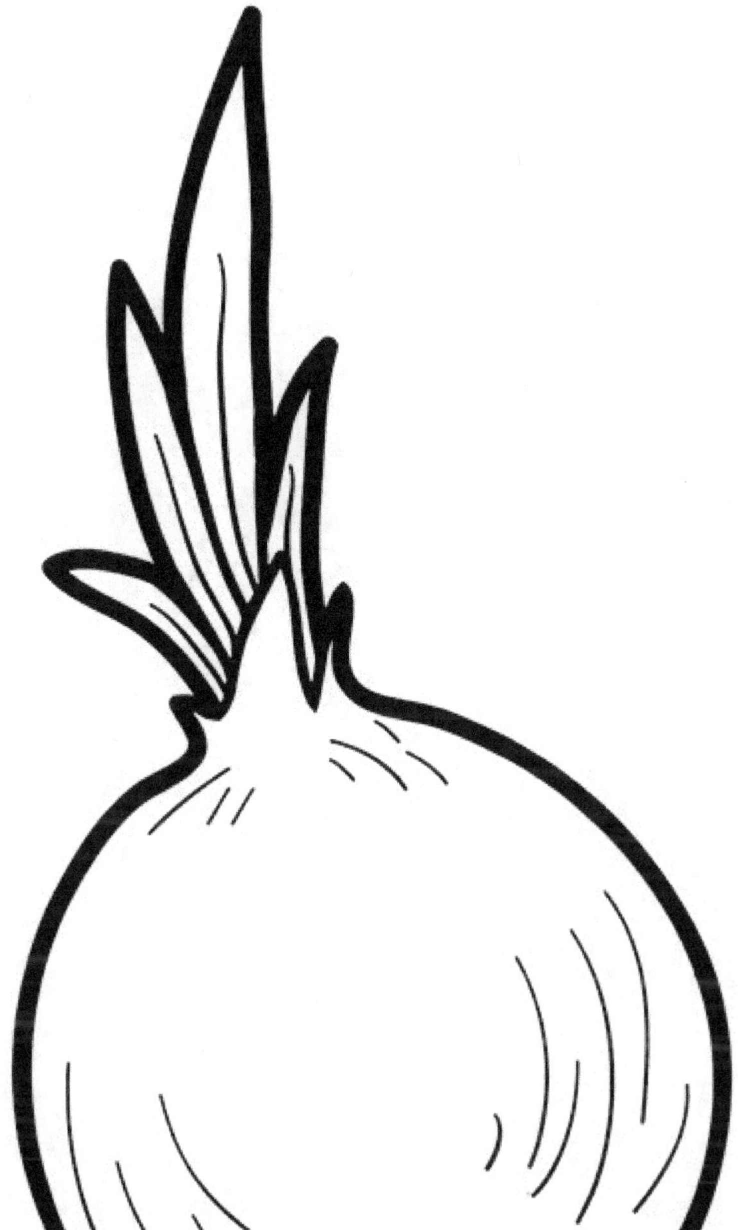

ONION

www.ingramcontent.com/pod-product-compliance
Lightning Source LLC
Chambersburg PA
CBHW082225220526
45470CB00010B/3314